PEOPLE ON SUNDAY

Geof
O'Bri

ffrey G

en

Peop
on
Sund

le

ay

WAVE BOOKS SEATTLE AND NEW YORK

Published by Wave Books

www.wavepoetry.com

Wave Books titles are distributed to the trade by

Consortium Book Sales and Distribution

Phone: 800-283-3572 / SAN 631-760X

This title is available in limited edition hardcover

directly from the publisher

Library of Congress Cataloging-in-Publication Data

O'Brien, Geoffrey G. (Geoffrey Gordon), 1969–

People on Sunday / Geoffrey G. O'Brien.—First Edition.

pages cm

ISBN 978-1-933517-77-3 (limited edition hardcover)

ISBN 978-1-933517-72-8 (trade paperback; alk. paper)

I. Title.

PS3615.B75P46 2013

811'.6—dc23

2012046702

Designed and composed by Quemadura

Printed in the United States of America

9 8 7 6 5 4 3 2 1

First Edition

Wave Books 036

FOR JEFF CLARK

PEOPLE ON SUNDAY

Four Last Songs

The sound was like picking sad battles,
The red that white imagines yellow is.

It was the sound of forgetting what
To do with the senses, being equally

Surprised by a voice subsiding, come
Slowly back, or edging toward actual close.

I'd forgotten to pay attention for years
To a song I heard for the first time

At the end of a recent memorial,
An actual song by Strauss about going

To sleep, predicting one's own death, etc.
Let me say this: I was surprised it kept

Going then surprised that it ended.
This was always true but could be more so

Much like those years of not knowing
The song felt brought back now

As inattention to its presence then.
And there are many versions

Of *Four Last Songs* and of this one,
As many as there are people

Who've made and played them.
Each one stands as someone's else,

The color of fading color, lastness
Pluralized because going to sleep

Keeps redoing the translation
Without fully having done. But this

Only applies to "Beim Schlafengehen"
From the *Four Last Songs* of Strauss.

At the Edge of the Bed

No one yet has ever chosen misery
Those that seem to have done so
Haven't any more than they have
Chosen this mist or is it rain

We would first have to own ourselves
Then give up on them entirely
Every day rather than once
And for all (which would be to seem

To have done so and not at all)
Like mist we speak of misery
In dissolves that don't, disappearances
That can't exactly be detected

That are not for detection by those
Senses we reliably seem to have
Is it your fault you don't yet
Use your time, all of it, to defend

Weather against those wishing
To control it, if only by letting it
Be amplified in its present effects?
No one wants the wave to come

Though some don't mind if it does
The question still what divides
The misery before it from that right
After, other than the wave itself. No

One listens to misery as if
Having chosen others over
Owning a private sunlight
Rays that touch people mid-conversion

Keep it from coming at all
Happiness too hasn't yet occurred
I mean are you kidding
Really nothing has but also

Nothing to some degree has not
Impossible to detect where one
Shades into the other so that
If I'm happy the sun wins

Through all that overcast have I
Forgotten the misery of others
Allowed its wave to break
On what the mornings expected

Had them happen to me without
Choice while also full of how
Sunlight comes all the time
Whether it can be detected

Regardless of what it alights on
It is a verb without intention
In a world unhappy with objects
You can't have it or choose not to

Still time to convert though
Not really from, not quite to
A misery intransitive as when
Sunlight takes a building

Thanatopsis

Here again just a few minutes
To see what we've done with what they let us have.
Like spring in Washington, D.C.
The way we're taught to imagine days

As reprieves from other days, cherries snowing
Inexpressiveness, the nation's capital
An experience of how it is to be
Caught up in pink and white again.

This year is somewhat different
In that there are very few days,
They have names like N9 and M1,
What they've let us do with what they can't

Keep us from having, a stand your ground
Law to address weeks of solid rain,
The street that goes on where the way is closed
Responding to events as they spread

From each instance to the live rule
Requiring them like spring requires
Trees to flower at points along their branches.
Today is M22, a private garden

And a public square, the path between them
Traced by daylight saving time
Over the freedom of George Zimmerman.
Like his ability to move in fantasy,

Certain days don't stop but shed
New ends continuously, as though
In lives not defined by the clock
Of limited resources. Other days

Not yet here—a greater scarcity
Of water, the first of the new kind
Of arrests—already reach back
Through their inevitability

Into potentials of the present tense,
The stare of passersby as you make
A viewing party of yourself, shouting
Drop the charges stemming from N9

On the one hand, while on the other
Wanting Zimmerman in chains
Beyond the room in which he finds himself.
Meanwhile the purple no one saw fall

Dotting the concrete outside my house
Like a pattern unpursued doesn't seem
To leave the paulownia any barer,
A participant in day but temporarily

Immune. As the resources disappear
There will be several such readjustments
But will they be chosen or imposed? Probably
The latter then the former then both

Going on together like towers,
Working in tandem without looking up
To see what day it is or was
They ruin time while we have it.

Materia

1

I had three tasks: finish, cease, and stop.
I had the single method: wait like form
On the inside of the outside, made
Of being made. There space is nothing
So large as, tests don't end they resume,
The good and bad have the same structure.
Let me be more specific: during the war
I remained unreal in order to match
The conflict's absence of termination
Or my experience of being involuntary
Went decisional, non-native grasses in the park,
Patterns at the edges of the game.
Or I joined one moment of helplessness
To another so that a perpetual intimacy

Spanned them, defeating time by further
Dividing it into nameless parts relation

Obtains among. This stretch in which
I washed the dishes perpetually affecting
This other where sunlight was done to me.
It's as though April were a permanent event
Green only briefly promotes, and vice
Versa, the opposite of clustered munitions;
Hapless, mostly hapless, and enduring.
Things that endure are not things.
They tend to show up in religions,
Both transforming and transformed until
Nearly indistinct from days, a joke
That points more to its author than the
Category errors on which it depends.
During the war I obtained April.

2

True, I had a single task: vary the method.
I taught others to watch helplessly
As May became the later months.
The tint of the peach deepens to disease,
The laptop makes an extra whirring sound
As in the stadium wrappers blow. Let me
Be much more specific here: I who
Had never understood classical music
Began to have feelings again, could not
Understand them except as the outside
Enduring the inside, thingless quick-
Slow-quick the good and bad are in
Transition through, passing the same
Sounds in different moral directions
(It was November, for instance, but hot).

When listening to music without drums,
Which is my definition of the classical,
When listening to how it erases the difference

Between those who gather and those still dispersed,
You feel the net become a door or bed,
You touch a cold stove without
An ash of consequence and pleasure is like
Being chased for no crime, done
With all those trivial shapes of things
From the autumn of every again.
Let the third half fall between you
Until minor bombs and defective chords
Worship at identical altars. One thing
We know: in finishing ceasing stops
Via a set of collectable reverberations.

3

Could they have used the other dispersant,
Could the lacquer be spread more evenly
Along the rim of the bowl the fruit lies
Helplessly in? Yes, but this is the west
Of all possible worlds, maternal as August,
And this is a four-letter word for assuming
You have enough data to continue angrily
Honoring your commitments, make
Anything a musical instrument, search
The stations for one of your friends,

The one both hapless and perpetual
Because listening to the *Kindertotenlieder*
Of Mahler. Now test what you've gathered,
You must not keep the night inside you
Distinct from the war on April, you must
Be the child, now dead, Pound heard
Ask its mother if it could open the light,
Which, because it was said without drums,

I would call classical, without end;
But then my parents died for years

Because their child had, much as trains
Run all the way to the stadium, airport, or beach.
Soon, when the storm hits, and friends are
Thrown into further circumstance,
There will be ways to visit them all at once,
Live like space, the opposite of stoppages.
But Monday, the worst kind of violin,
The most unflattering light in which to appear,
Also lives in this remotest of intensities
Feeling plays where the year won't hear it.

4

The poem excluding history includes it,
Like saying "It's 76 degrees and money"
Before stepping outside or deciding to
Say it's Thursday, autumn of the week,
Whether or not it is, ends recycling
Through other ends. The sun shines
Because the workweek desires it
Or because it desires the week be lit,
No information external to the scene,
None within, the task of the peach at dusk
A version of the joke about everything,
The one about the other one,
Reverberations that can't be told apart
Yet I'm confident they're going to be
Like Stevens and Stein and stadium lights.

Could the outside have gone otherwise,
Are beaches free of oil, can you marry a drum of it
By connecting nothing inside to the nothing

Without? Yes, but not how you mean that,
There are rules and rules are like ice
In the sun. Form is a child of deathsong,
Parentless, there will soon be ways
To visit all at once. In the meantime tasks
Unstoppably haunt the body, days
Nothing so great as a feeling comes;
You feel confident saying it's going
To rain but not when, you feel certain
Your job is to be mad but not at,
Method without object, object the subject
You wanted to be here but not like this,

5

This has nothing to do with it.
You are responsible for each sunset's
Likeness to the end of the world,
Chopped-up cheerfulness that is
The sign of its formal relation to war
Or how camouflage changes over time,
Each with its historical season of
Use and late transition in
To uselessness, accompanied by drums.
Could they have refrained? Varied
Their method of ceasing, a poem for once
Modeled on conflict resolution only in
The manner the sunset is, light exchanged
For lights, could they for they could?
About this question I'm neutral the way
The cat is about the house, the way

150 lines on the usury of weather
Fall through no space perpetually.

Yet I feel confident. Like iron in autumn
There are rules. The first movement comes
Before the other three and is called
A sonata, its task to move into the slow
Wartime of the adagio, which is about it
The way money is a form of weather
Poetry, world-joke whose origin is lost
In the traces minor chords preserve.
Nor does it end there among the invasive
Grasses, in a million-pillared symphony
So called because of the forces required
To perform it, but I'm confident it could.

D'Haussonville

A town no one lives in
Must be everywhere around us
Accounting for the hysteria
Of any pose. As we see into
The laugh of things fields or folds
Of wrinkled blue appear divided
Into secondary propositions
Of a primary fact, that fronts are lighter
Than backs because attention glows
And the body offered for inspection
Tries to master this overlit house
By pointing up specific parts,
One hand at the neck pulse while
The other wraps or reprises the waist.
None of which should be visible
In the mirror behind but is, nor should
Flowers grow up out of the dark
Of the back but they do, for centuries

Now without getting any larger.
It doesn't help that the right arm around
Her waist seems to grow from her torso
Rather than her underwhelming shoulder
Or that the left arm's elbow drives
Up from resting on the right hand,
Intent on ending in a hand of its own,
Which surrounds and supports the canted chin
Only by indicating it exists in space.
I happen to know for a nonfact
It was raining on this particular day
So no reason to have the face
Display any obvious flowers
Of an agony collected everywhere
Beyond the frame in Haussonville,
Where it only rains outside,
Where Ingres set off the entre nous
As a repopulated network of the glance
Figured also in the interior monologue
The surface of her body causes. You
Can see the modern prison forming too
If you close her eyes, which are and are not
Looking at you, a glance with two fronts,
Two backs, a front and a back, or a half.

"That's where she lacks support" (overheard
On the 51B at College and Alcatraz)
But I trust support is there, a past
Of intentional oil spills across canvas.
It was flowering out that endless day,
Writing down a copy of the red,
Pink, yellow, and white of other
Days, each the only example
At hand. And no matter who you are
She is bemused and pessimistic
Your damage can see her padded hurt
Though by her I mean the hand of Ingres
To which both of hers invisibly point
Throughout. This is happening and not
Happening, like the things in a mirror
Whose frame escapes the picture's own
And has a candle-sconce attached to it
But no candle, not even an unlit one,
So daylight and the phantom presence
Of a forgetful servant who could have been
Called by the blue bellrope closely
Tracking down that part of the mirror's gilt
Frame the painting allows us to see.
What else do we ever know but that

Torsos sitting on hips the way pots
Cut flowers have been dropped in rest
On credenzas themselves covered in blue velvet
Are what is only partially occluded here.
It's been done before; even admitting
It's been done before's been done, but not
In Haussonville, where it rains supports
Of all kinds, and variations on blue,
Enough to populate a sitting room
The single figure richly parses,
Trapped in what has been called
A rainbow of blues, deep but narrow
Luxury reflected in a mirror
Into which you can and can't possibly be seeing
Accurately. She would go on to write
Romantic novels and historical studies
Without her left hand ever leaving
Her chin, the chin of a great-granddaughter
Of Louis XVI's finance minister, Necker,
The last Comptroller General of Finances
Of the Ancien Régime. It is 1842
But is this Paris or Haussonville? Yes,
But there's more, because she is further
The granddaughter of Mme de Staël

So that all this trivial importance stacks
Behind her glowing face like the eighty
Studies Ingres made for the portrait,
Including sixty for the gown alone,
While the many blues of the painting
Pass into and out of the uniform shade
The revolutionary army's soldiers wore,
Now reduced to the "storm of approval"
With which the painting was received
By friends and family. She also wrote
A biography of Byron, which her gown
Has already begun in its pleats.
Like the dream of seeing hidden things
And the hugest processes therein
The blue only refers, is "of," genetic
And hard to kill off. It is 1845
Forever when the painting is completed
Though she herself is no longer
Twenty-four or anatomically
Incorrect as he has made her here.

Series

Wood is useless, nothing can be done with it.
It lies there like a person to whom
You've proposed working in exchange
For inessential goods. She has always said no,
There still isn't a way to divert her
From the needs whose satisfaction makes her
Perennially happy. Time too is
Indivisible into manageable units
That would be faithfully observed
By an undissenting populace
Like holidays or laws, whatever those are,
And there is as yet no populace.

Distraction

Spenser coined *blatant* to show us the scandal
Of truth can only be invented. The same
Holds true for you, in whom subject and object
Sound alike a common depth, "the never other
Than lost continuity" Grossman defines
As present wherever poems are present.
Stein says "They will not nearly know"
As if she were one of the Romantics
But is not talking about a ruin or frieze.
What is she talking about? The etymology
Of *blatant*, which has caused speculation
Precisely because it was coined. The fact
That Spenser used it to modify "beast"
Makes its kinship with *blaitand*, "bleating"
In 16th c. Scots, appealing, but the Latin
Blatire, "to babble," also makes sense
In context. Stein is blatant, especially
In *Stanzas in Meditation*, from which

The quotation above comes, as does
"You should never be pleased with anything."
Both quotes address the you of poetry
At a point where knowing and pleasing
Lose their hold. This is the faith
Behind the wager of the 18th-century
Actor Richard Daly, who believed the mind
Of the Irish to be so perfectly athwart
The subjective and objective states
That he was willing to bet "A word
Of no meaning should be the common talk
And puzzle of the city in twenty-four hours;
In the course of this time the letters Q, U,

I, and Z were chalked or pasted on all the walls
Of Dublin with an effect that won the wager."
The etymology of *quiz* is blatant, that
Of *blatant* quizzical, which is not the case
With *stanza*, clearly from "dwelling" or "room"
In the Romance languages but really
From *stāre*, to stand. So when Stevens
Writes *"stanza my stone"* he is asking
That Stein be made into a place to stand
For poetry, but of whom does he ask this?

For Grossman the answer is staring you
In the face while for Spenser it's under
The dragonskin of community.
It must be relentlessly tested, even
Forgotten then resurrected, haunting
Poems like the floating face of *Absalom,*
Absalom! that accompanies Sutpen down
Off the mountain into an understanding
Of class. Dragon Skin is also the name
For a type of flexible body armor produced
By Pinnacle, made of high tensile ceramic
Discs arranged in an imbricated overlapping
Configuration then encased in an aramid
Textile cover. There's a Level V variant
Not available to the general public,
But the public needs no protection
So long as it stays general. Not that it does,
Unfortunately, especially in Stein,
Where "in changing it inside out nobody
Is stout." Her poem babbles on
Until you live in the rooms of Grossman's account
Of Crane's "The Broken Tower," a poem
He argues is about vocation, another calling.
Here is a wall and some chalk.

From Honey to Ashes

What follows is terms and classifications, the West
Of speech congratulating itself within
A system so complex there's no way not to be
Effective. Just as they had planned, the streets
On either side are lined with all that's needed,
Storefronts whose glass returns a look
Filled with the contents it displays
(Mannequins, organics, mobile phones)
Making even moving sitting still, embrace
Above anything that's so. Cuts and clouds
Drift south across the far part of the sky
From adventure to instruction, so where
There's only the mildest threat of showers
You see a shape and then a story, parody
Of the private life of the world.
And what was promised to the mind of the hearer
In transformation remains away, ideal

Portrait there is a certain pleasure in reading
As buffer against what today sends tomorrow.
It's like forgetting that part of childhood
In which one learned to do everything
From the pages of a book not unlike
A painting, but a painting with motion
In its idle depths, down where dusk meets
Foreclosure and the clouds charge out
Into the gift of seeing them forthrightly
Pass by a thing that might have happened, public
Pleasures that progress, the horizon, etc.
Always more or less just starting out
Its day, though it would be better to call it
A grouping sent down through suffering
To sunset, signed in the same place each time
To win over the jury in advance; it's a painting
Of the burning of a book whose content is
Disputed: colors, lights, fragments
Taken from the wound, greater and lesser
Distances, all read to tell bad from good,
Grant the fading premises in every sense.
What follows is seven dominated days
Of the week ready to bind with really anything

At all, your thoughts as you come forward
Out of the haze like sun through a curtain
Or go to sleep so as to be of further use —
Till sight doesn't feel like buying houses
Aren't these one and the same task?

Suleiman

A simple poem would be content traveling
Back from the future to transfer its burden
Of knowledge about the present, but this one
Stays in that present, unable to see
Anything beyond the overrun square.

Or mistakes seeing for having just talked,
Waits there with permanent demands.
That one too is ultimately simple,
As simple as having something to say
About death (it's partially total),

As simple as Egypt if Egypt were
To live forever on the edges of the square
(Twenty years from now the square is gone).
The complex poem admits all this
From a counterpresent the future denies

All knowledge of, where talking looks
Like seeing and seeing writes it down
Whether or not in the order it should
It comes. The peaceful transfer of
Power from the past to the future

Sees the end of a present, escorted
By sand. It's also the complex poem
Made simple, so that everyone can
Use it as easily as a banner
And the crowd a crowd of conductors

(In twenty years the poem will be music)
For a time held wide enough open
We are the palm trees near the beach
Whose edges are ragged and not yet
Deserted. And then there is

The compound poem, what happens when
The simple and complex meet
In the middle distance of live feeds,
A wind in the palms. Totally at last
The present is all talking parts.

Tales of Unrest

My control over passing
Clouds remains
Imperfect, and a power
To hold back the desert

Flowers of Nevada—White
Rhatany, Scented Cryptantha,
Cinchweed, Canterbury
Bells, Showy Goldeneye—fails

In their coming irrevocably
Early, for the same reason
The face must be shielded
From both sun and protest

But forgive others for what
They're bound to say next,
In the name of something
Or out of a need, because

Their nation somehow also
Produces *My Life*, "The King-
Fishers," "At Night
The States," "Crossing Brooklyn

Ferry," "Into the Dusk-Charged
Collected Poems of
The second person's Oscar
Grant Plaza, friends

I ran through the smoke of
With Susan and Sri,
The latter of whom I don't
Know well enough to name,

On January 7—past
Its mostly sunny high
Of 48 dropping to a low
Of 35, NDAA and H.R.

347, the boy momentarily
Atop a police cruiser—
Toward the next day's
Coward flower.

The best things train us
For what you have to
Get, can only get
From complete strangers

Who aren't by the time
You do. Do what
Exactly, with *the* not yet
A synonym for *our*

And *our* still pouring
Through the articles
Declaring it's over and you
Didn't do enough if

You is I, whom we don't
Know sufficiently to run,
Only wake up as, committed
To having four while needing

Five, whatever it is they are,
The whole collectable set
Bid on without auction,
Funny expectations

Almost like survival
If survival were exposed
Roots stumbled over on a path
In places if places depend

On having the patience
To keep going back, spend
Entire days without
Hours, rub a broken clock

In the hopes that
Or until such time as
But for the moment
And soon, very soon

The lantana suddenly
Blazes like surveillance,
Unpredictable device
Heading through the warmest

Driest wettest weather
On record everywhere but here,
Drought and floods
Flowering at the same time

Between now and then,
Sent across the present's
Face while unnoticeably
Disastrous possibilities

Having already happened
Still float down
In particles of something
You have to get through

These lines to catch
In the others where its
Antecedent might, neither
Early nor late, finally

Appear, friendly stranger
You remember briefly having
Spoken with but little
If any of what we said.

Series

Now that I want to talk to you we are
Facing the disgust of the soloist
That he even has to
Banish the rest of them
I understand the pleasure lies
In being headed up a ramp
Made mostly of conjecture
One has a say in stopping
I understand the conductor's gone
Who regulates these things
Before the strings begin
So here is where he makes
Sounds that go only so far
Along a bridge collapse
Long and short remains
Sneering through the instrument
I understand the pleasure lives

In lace not meant to be worn
In accepting invitations
To stand just outside a circle
Come all those miles to

Hesiod

There is another time for men to sail in the spring.
As soon as the size of the crow's footprint is matched
by the aspect of the leaves on the end of the fig-
branch, then the sea is suitable for embarcation.
WORKS AND DAYS

All songs at once, isn't this
Like balancing the needs of friends?
He who emits a voice must think
About those streams already running.
The middle of the month especially,
Its pallets and sleds, false Sundays
Convened with morning coffee pride
Spreading out as powers felt
In turning on the background sounds.
The month lies further
Divided into weeks, which will have
A habit of encroaching, and what was all

Dark circles of potential in the hand
Or a nearly transparent green
Floating just outside the obvious soon
Falls back to familiar hours
Designed for a desert capital
Where to wander unaccosted
Has become a form of genius.
And the fragrance curling around
The casement window is forgotten
Appointments with fallow surfaces
In a room so small or consistent
It has the demeanor of distance.
Those glints far off are steadying
Instances of everything's arc
While flashes near at hand present
Alarms you tirelessly survive
By noting almost immediately
They can be discounted. Just that
Much more web texture, yellow
Of the green lime leaves going away
Like a process. Self-interested
Exchanges, robberies on holiday,
The best that can be said is
They devolve like blasted tones

From generations on the wane,
They have good tumble and fade, a currency
You run the risk of being taken for.
So when the jacaranda starts
Dropping flowers underneath the helicopter
And everything says it all,
Give them back their money utterly.
But morning again, funny this
Should happen now, and shoddy
Elevations failing in all directions
But the one that matters, day trading
Up from infinitive to imperative,
Isn't that a history of breakfast told
To amoral wrens, the inability to move
To larger quarters while the givens
Hold their ground? Typically
The last few days of the month respond
In the affirmative, exhausted yellows
Ready for the next. Make no appointments
At this time, when hate is liable
To come for you in the guise of free
Chairs left out on the street,
Use these mornings like they are
Communicating rooms calls come from,

Sometimes your mother, sometimes
Your stepmother, and be mindful
Of unofficial anniversaries
In the leaves of the sickly apricot.
From the 27th to the 28th rest
In embarrassing determinations:
Dressed before you leave the house,
Give no credence to initial thoughts
That round things love form more
Than angled ones. Wait mindless
As an herb. Leave your kitchen, the dome
Of performances, carrying out
No advice specific enough
To help you. Fear all wheeled cars,
Indifferent when near, a gloss stream
Where the sidewalk falters. Their speed
Would seem to indicate you don't exist
Unless your job's to tear old sheets
All day, no that's the sound they make
Driving in March rain. This is spring,
Building with a single entrance, and the peace
Invading your boots, isn't that
Sunday too, a form of bestowing
Useful when the senses offer up

Their measurements of that which is
Imagined lost? But from the 1st
To the 4th space will involve you
In gradual commitments, packaging
Materials there long after the fact
Has laid out half the audience.
I'd like instead a total serum
To change the hue of conversations
You have with those same days
The man is selling subscriptions for
Despite the mist or is that rain
Coming down unscheduled. If not
Handing over anything, if it occurs to you
Anyway to drop the changing blade
You didn't know you held, have held too long,
Then do so, it won't lose its edge
On what passes here for pavement.
Instead of that lost sound
Which would end your usual pursuits
You hear him ring the neighbor's bell,
Signal to host the deadening thoughts
And her greeting, it's from out of another
World, strange setups and pleasures
Timed to coincide with getting up.

But sleep, the better part
Of sleep is do nothing till morning
Throws some dead coats again,
Spells a few letters with your limbs
Underneath the sheets of a climate
That rewards and then withdraws.

In your house you can refuse to
Answer the door, pretend you aren't up,
But at a meeting nod just as often
As those around you seem to do.
Maintain eye contact while sitting down,
Pretend there are no weapons in the air,
Be the first to offer a dry hand
If departure seems likely, and tie
Each cloned vine to its pole
While listening, reduce the rich traffic
To notes: there may be other incidents
For which the present moment is practice.
Talking will tend toward spill or relief,
Green rays around the head
Mistaken for foliage or ideas
Of money even further abstracted,
But do it anyway, this is the spring

Crowds are led to all year, only
House available at the moment
So you'll have to move again. Good times
To buy with confidence are the 12th
And 17th, especially to purchase
Your things, the socks that go inside
The boots, liquids got at through
The tops of bottles. There is in fact
No choice but shop on days that end,
Half-convinced paying is stealing
And you are again capable of thinking
In a queue sunset seems to question
Through the storefront, gently efface
In a manner suggestive of waves. Yet
Don't confuse the figure waiting
On the bed for you with property,
The senses with instruction. Neither stay
Nor flee but list the unavailable
Pauses rain again falls out of
Like tinsel, how he or she avoids it
Anyway, preferring circumstance.
Neglected by unwanted catalogues,
Sales that come when far too many
Others already have, live as if

Oil in water or only in
Noon, early February, month they haven't
Figured out yet. To arrive or leave it
Dragging involuntary wares, how bad
Is that? Isn't it like having songs
Suggested to you, backing up slowly
Though there are no cars? Yes
But a persistent sense remains
Of trades, boards, being the last to know,
Figures returned to not as they were left,
The light still on, whole houses of it
To either side modeling what
You should do: go home and lie there
On the first Sunday of the month,
Ambitious as a phone in the grass
While April prematurely comes
To grief, entrance without a building.
In May prepare yourself for bouts
With inadvertent comedy, a further breath
For every one exhaled, second nature
By the time your interlocutor appears,
Floats back in as though used to this.
What is it allows them to drive everywhere
Through a fabric without back,

To understand machines right away?
They've lived a second life inside the first
Like a shade you should replace? Look
Them in the eye and admit you are
Still on the first of many cups. But when
The shadow of the woman in a housecoat
Standing on the porch next door
Reaches to the storm drain and
The number on the curb is freshly painted red
Go out, space will not insult you.
This is the spring sailing through,
An old man standing in the bushes
Calling in some favors. I don't recommend it
Though you could do much worse
Than walking past the empty stores.
The sky might unlike possessions
Open up at any time, remember that
Even chance thoughts become nets
When dealing with acquaintances
At the season's first official function.
Better yet, consider staying in
A hinted realm extending days until
The rains stop and the cable van is parked
Beneath the sycamore. Full summer now,

A sound like sleepy song, the commerce
Unintended in trucks on a bridge
Too far away to see them really
But they must be there, commands
Already followed as loyally as
The window sticks you're trying quite
Properly to open. Do not at 10 a.m.
While early heat flows tenderly in
Imagine that a pattern forms in how
Drab birds fly by like news, typical
Shadows this time of year. Hold out
For another hour at least, remain
Embarrassed there were ever kings.
Kill with consultation those you usually
Do — it's as much your fault as it is
Not that the brew was overstrong.
And the mailtruck now approaching,
Show it no hope; don't let comfort
Arrest you or have your thinking
Become an oblong offering:
Anything sealed behind a pane
Would make you sad to see. Then you
Remember she called you, won't really
Be alive until the siren in the middle

Distance stops testing your doors,
But don't call back lightly, this
Leverage grows only while unused.
Wait at least until the sun is in
The anchorman's eyes, till halftime
When the cars start up an evensong.
You'll never get a better opportunity
Than early June, days like gems
Loose from settings largely unchanged
In half a century; you can tell it's here
By the tightness dispersing in the chest
Just before speech explains
Your best work is still behind you.
Therefore be masters of the dew,
Specialize in everything the way
The days proceed. And think of them
As dupes crashing in on each other
Despite its being more than clear
They pose in adjacent displays,
Monday and Tuesday especially
But all the others as well, Mondays
By another name. It takes weeks
To learn how to use a negative space
Effectively. When the markets close

You feel time flows differently inside
Then you may close the book and drive,
Full of arid conflicts. Isn't this
The lesson of ivy on a broken wall
The neighbor shares, casual tracings out
Through acquisitiveness too slow
For an eye to catch progress? It seems
To grow in units of sleep but not
Even that much nightly connection
Can be responsibly imagined. Turn
To your associations, check the afternoon
Of the 6th and 9th for lurching faces,
the 11th for the bodies underneath them.
Dancing is anger made good
While a rival marks the opportunity to speak
Passed up yet somehow heard.
You wouldn't want to manage his estate
But drifting through a lonely game
Of unrelated terms, imagining crowds
To be simple plots of environment,
Seems equally arranged. Sea laps tanker
As oil coats rock and the rich man is he
Who attaches no name to public works
And refrains from loving anything.

Mark

There was nothing but days. Seven
Box stores set along the broken way
Filled with generation. And the people
Came to each as the other six days
Of being amazed. At first thirty or so,
Not enough to survive in
Or anything else. Enough to run

The first person through a face
Surrounded and brought comparison.
A month cut and paved with squares
So Sundays could occur, free to keep
If you like such things. The main point
To be coming home then leaving
Again, led on by anonymous promises

Into fluorescence and particleboard,
Coated wire, sugar, smart and self-
Circulating waters, heated cups,
Mountain men in a world without
Mountains. Hidden hours headed
Toward then against but little in the way
Of raw materials. Convenient the trap-beds,

Convenient the house shakes if
The truck is full. Privately they
Brought the head to be heard but it
Counts for nothing while alive. Instead
No voice said here are companies,
Cut flash, instruments designed
To produce inviting distances; we won't

Reject you, you'll be heard both
Coming and going, sit down and eat,
Come apart and gather in, ask what is
Tolerable, a house the purse far time
Passes. They said it asleep in tombs,
Both sorry and pleased items went
With them to the next domain

But one. And they came to fall,
The days, like gifts without sense. Within
There was nothing but deaf coast, heads
On strings, bills for hands, a house
They were commanded to dream
Was missing nothing but more.
And they were good at swapping

Surnames for possessions, night for day
Cycling past with its messenger bag,
All things published or possessed
In a kind of recirculation seen by any
Everyone. And since the face is made
Of little warm circuits, half-real
Charities friends will rely on, sleep

Now flows like electrical current.
So mechanical the calm about perishing
You'd think an order had been given
To assume the city was always there
In silent commute, and they took to the maze,
Rotating through assaulted exchange
What they could say any of them would.

Entheogen

Ariana, there's the utopia
Of misrecognition, and the one
Of recognizing that. Paradise is
Neither of these if neither were
More nearly a positive term.
Joanna says paradise is not
A domain but the plan for imagining
A future of returns. The closest
I've come was in New Mexico
When a horned toad I surprised
Forced blood from its eye
Into my face as I stood on the edge
Of De Maria's lightning field.
That part of the country has always
Seemed to me something other
Than potential real estate, there are
So few signs of a human present
Or its past, enough absences that

It's the neither of nature and culture,
Dust hanging in the air.
I should admit I was sent there
Alone by plane several times as a child
In the '70s to visit my uncle, then
Curator of the Navajo museum
In Santa Fe, and I've always loved
Uncles, that mix of brother and father
Also a flight out of the immediate
Family (cf. Eve Kosofsky
Sedgwick) that doesn't require leaving it,
So they may be the neither of family
Because nearly full of its terms,
And my uncle Steven therefore
Might have enchanted the red clay
Further out of its genocidal calm
Already posing as deep previousness
And an underdevelopment falling
With the rain visible fifty miles away,
Uneventfulness like being
Constantly blasted by no harm; but really
Recognizing that mistake does not
Dissolve the effect or desire to return
There, which I never do. Because

Of how America is, though America
Isn't the name for the problem,
You said you wanted a talk on paradise
In poetry, to be given at your thing
In Santa Fe. Paradise is unbounded
Enclosures as little present
In any stretch of poetry
As New Mexico is in the States,
It flickers in and out of the majuscule
Until "The hand holds no chalk" to draw
Its location, as the poet wrote in his self-
Portrait from the city of my birth,
Though he saw it in Vienna in '59
With Pierre Martory, for once really himself
Though getting ready to depart,
Or neither himself nor not. Joanna
Considered using J.A. on paradise
As an epigraph to her book but balked
Finally at the anachronism
Though the anachronistic may be
A sign paradise is near, putting
Good pressure on the immediate
Like an uncle outside Taos.
I still haven't sent you her book,

Which is about a practical program
For restoring Eden in the Seventeenth
Century as the collective subject
Of science or literature, any truth-
Producing group. This is apt now
As well, not just because of Occupy
But because now is in time even if
It seems not to be in New Mexico when
Staring at the dwellings of first inhabitants.
I worry you won't read Joanna's work
Until neither is a verb, and nothing
I'm saying is new though I haven't said it
Before, nor addressed you (who are
In love with the dust of the second person),
And I haven't captured the New
Mexico that attracted D. H. Lawrence
And André Breton, coming closest
Maybe when evoking Los Alamos
In the past tense via "blasted" above.
This land was always postnuclear,
Out of time while in it. You've written
About Truth and Consequences,
New Mexico, so you know and have
Your own version, your inspired tactical

Reasons for picking N.M. as a place
To think in, a place to invite
Those with whom you want to imagine
Restoring the world as functional
Subject of interdisciplinary whatever
You decide you want together, however
Briefly. But it isn't Truth and Consequences,
It's Truth *or* Consequences, I truly
Made that mistake then really recognized it;
Replacing *or* with *and* marks
The kind of parapraxis paradise
Causes where it can't appear,
Sort of like how I nearly came to your thing,
How I should have come
And you should have had it in Oakland.

Second Intensity

I stood in Pound's fake spring 100 years
Later, pessimistic the continuous
Renovations are really for us,
Mistaking thinking this for joining

A tradition of finding each other
Through laments we're unavailable,
Bad light on the time-killing face
Anonymous as a pomegranate.

Translation: I took the underground
Brooklyn ferry to the past while waiting
For a train, pretended I could count
Mosaic, tally the work they had done

In navy and cream tiles for the three of us
Then five ranged along the platform
Never satisfied with being
A general petal of our privacy.

Observation: it's embarrassing
Still to be riding this system, antiquated
As reading a newspaper or choosing
The semicolon, looking into a face

Rather than at it; and the oldest thing,
Talking silently to the other strangers,
Which I've been doing seven minutes
Now into a lack of encouragement.

Anyway: in a can't-win world
I hear you out against dull roar
As the minimum of sustenance
Though you aren't exactly talking

But somehow enough while seeming not
To be anywhere close. We met once
Or was it every time, hard to say
When the crowd closed its eye, the door

Opened onto stations slick
With succeeding. You grew accustomed
To light below ground, somewhere between
Tradition and addiction as it makes you

Legitimate again. It's like the last time
Never ended and you forgot
To be more than looped postures,
Temporary lights in their yellow baskets

That when you look at them are the eyes
Anything is, the eyes we bring
To spring's green stanchions unaware
They're become or becoming

Part. And forgive me for adding you
When you're just the faintest example
Of empire stress at the other end
Of the poem, with the F due in two minutes

While you lean against the freshly painted
Faith it will come, water on the tracks
Patient as a rat. There are so many
Of you, that's what right now means,

Chances lost before their apprehension
Yet all the same continuing.
You get the feeling your being at risk
Doesn't require a definite event,

Could close back down into routine
Like being bathed and carried once was.
Now you've gone from remembering
Not having to ask for that care

To walking down worn-out steps
With a soft dip in their middle
Without much of a protest.
You shouldn't be able to

Be here where everything is out of place
And even variety looks typical
But there is no making things
Happen faster. It's the opposite

Of dreaming except that objects
Are alive and episodic, connected
By comforting blurs. And just the two
Of us now, alone with the signs for scar

Repair and jobs on the force. I watched you
Ignore them all at once, do it
Like a veteran, shaking without moving,
Then forgot myself in the same way.

People on Sunday (1930)

Now they really are involved, drinking
Coffee with the elms behind them. The trick
To wet the coiled paper slowly so the day
Expands like a writhing insect
As trash is swept up and the resultant street
Hosed down, not everyone free to brag
In the black and white sunshine.
It gets in the eyes of the mechanic during his
Rotations of the left front wheel
Spinning like the crowds around a monument.
Okay, fine, but what about tomorrow?
Done. The rest is knitting outdoors
Or no, she was petting a struggling cat
That from a distance looked to be
Complacent wool while she stood there.
Barge after barge follows this mistake
Along the major river she considers
While getting ready, starting with her nails,

But maybe she doesn't want to go out
Yet, ambivalence of lying back down
With one's shoes still on. Jacket off,
He's proud of his surroundings, the two
Bottles on a table by a single glass.
Amazingly, they are in the same apartment
Reading parts of one paper
By the inadvertent clock of a faucet
Leaking. It's not even Sunday yet
Nor are they actors, but it's time to change

Clothes, sweep the face with a lathered brush
By a wall with photographs of film stars on it.
You use scissors, I'll use razor and soap,
And for some reason we'll both go to work
Destroying their faces after having gone
To great lengths to collect and mount them.
It's a prelude to going out in our best
Or will they, maybe an argument about
How she's chosen to wear her hat first,
A bit of a scene in which more photographs
Get destroyed. Or forget photos actually,
We can play cards now that there are two men
Present and she'll have to watch

Sunday punish her without access to its images
Of smoke from a chimneystack, a man asleep
On a park bench, collective living
Pursued in a single bed. Only now
Is it Sunday. He wakes first and washes up,
Tries to rouse her somewhat roughly
But she is not yet there in the way he is
So he leaves a note by the cards and glasses
On the table at which he'd sat with the other
Man and goes. There are so many like him
Outside, and monuments, arches to be
Passed through in a car, and of course
The bridges, the smoke. That which can't be
Passed through or under can still be passed by,
Advertisements on the sides of apartments,
Windows, trains, and trees. They're all going
To the same unrevealed place, half an arrow.
Shy in the best-friend role, she looks down
Suddenly interested in tree-filtered light
On pavement. You go on, I must place
A phone call, walk down these endless stairs,
Buy a postcard, order a drink, pair off as
The whims of the atmosphere demand,
Carry a suitcase through the park

To its less populated places. In fact,
That's what my silent phone call is about,
That and whether she's even gotten out
Of bed or whether her shoes are still
Unoccupied. It turns out you can walk
All the way to a beach, where you'd take them off
Again to become the postcard of a bather
If no one saw you undress and change.
Now the suitcase makes sense, but not
That kind, it seems to be a portable
Device for playing music, music to change to
With clouds as inspiration. This is
Working out, there are definite foregrounds
And backgrounds, each composed
Then dissolving or stopping abruptly

Starting up again as though continuous
And yes, she's still in bed so you'll have to
Enter the water without her, splash of white
Where you just were. You, if you are still
The man on shore, help the other
Woman with her impossible suit and now
Your friendliness has a touch of eros to it,
You would wake her much less roughly

On that same part of the back of the shoulder
You targeted unsuccessfully this morning,
But this one's already awake and away,
You share a single body with the water
And forget. Swimming from becomes
Swimming toward, a flirtation through
The awkwardness of the element, and walking
Down steps requires they be walked back up,
Agreeable fate they greet as though air
Were water and vision. Whose desire
Is this anyway and is it a cloud or the boat
Beneath the cloud, the blanket or the sand
Beneath that or the thermos and bottles, etc.
If he won't move the other man will and if
He won't serve them sausages the other
Does till everyone's restored—losing some
Is okay because there's enough and it's not
Even lost—he cleans it off and eats it anyway.
Coughing and laughing, each can cause the other,
But laughing may last longer in a moment
While coughing goes on intermittently for days
Like a group of boys in ties who take turns
Striking each other. Who's next is more painful
Than the blows themselves, the same with goals

In sports or growing up into shame about
Your nakedness. Swimming the distance
From birth you're now used to experiencing
As water or Sunday, those two girls at a window
Fringed by oak trees. The other method to fall
Asleep on a park bench so that while clothed
You have no sense you are, or your trust in others
A nakedness your clothes wear and for a second
We can lie back upon the grasses partly
Nude, taking liberties we won't push too far.
We are as asleep as she who never left the bed,
Who sleeps for us all like a perfect actor.
Now the midafternoon when storefronts thrive,
Fountains rise a little higher, vision pans
Always to the left across construction sites,
Laundry hung out windows, public statues
(Men or animals) and even an obelisk
Crowds rotate around rather than confront
Their obvious destination. In time
It's all sand, even the marble, so smile
While holding still whether naked or not,
Knowing or not, fat with discomfort
Or aware it's a trap even when surprised

To know this. Those in front of a camera
Are missing in a saintly way, statues with lives.
Their smiles carry injury, their sadness a power
To adapt, say thank you to the worst of it,
Make a game of snatching its hat and running off
Throwing it till it lodges in one of the oaks.
This precipitates a whole other serious game
Of cooperation—at least three will be required
To spend time getting back the hat of only one,
An inefficiency permitted on Sunday,
The day groups form and learn from,
Deciding where within the frame to go next.
Before choosing a path touch your mouth,
Looking sadly at the available options,
Then take none at all except the space
Between young trees. Here you'll meet him
For a second but keep going, there are better
Places to stop for what will happen, and act
Surprised, even discouraged, when he behaves
Predictably; you do too, and where you touch
Each other proof will bloom you aren't trees
Growing out of sand. Head back to the right,
You can't go left forever; go up even, up and right

Then down to where he's standing while you
Fake sleep and waking from it. He looks as if
He's getting ready for work, holds a pinecone
Like it's an ancient tool. Others are similarly
Strewn through the instant's overexposure,
Sprawled or walking, trudging down embankments
Or headed back to the starting point. It's a huge park
Filled with time they are going to convene
Drowsily, close the musical briefcase, no, not yet,
First a kind of modular pairing-off known
As where are the others — it feels good to say
Finally, even if no answer is immediately
Forthcoming or has stopped to take something
Out of its shoe. The answer is they are here
One at a time. That feels good too, slanted
Light to play a last song on the portable
While the final straggler makes her reluctant
Way across involuntary terrain
Over to the fact of the rest. She almost got lost
And that almost is crucial, with its being time
To return, the blue of the afternoon darker
Or deeper, a fight about to break out. Pleasures
Have to be shared, and the grimness thereof

When they're about to fade. There are many
Others afterward; they keep falling through
The speed of any one activity's end
Into a paddleboat either sex can power

Without shame; it's even enjoyable to move
From passenger to operator and back,
Thinking or doing, melancholy or magnanimous.
The four have forgotten about those who are not
In their boat but are surrounded all the same
By shoreline with unlimited populations
Maples by the water represent; the men
Start play-hitting her, taking fake turns
As they near the shore, and she is mad and happy,
An oar in their water. It's time to remember, talk
Across greater distances, cooperate with strangers
Stranded nearby. We'll go over there and retrieve
For them what they can't get for themselves
Even if it makes us jealous of each other.
Sad to be connected to somebody by so little
So briefly, a note thrown in the water
Unfolds faster. Pedaling hard now they reach
A mooring that leads to others, structures
Of some kind where they will have to part

If not all have the money to go on, no, they can
Lend him the money to ensure they meet again.
And he is there, they're four and one,
It's still Sunday, full and orchestral if right
About to burn as well. The four become two
Men and two women thinking of the next
Sunday, and probably lying to each other
About this so their bodies will part for real.
One man breaks his cigarette in two to celebrate,
Gives half to the other man. They ride the tram
Like boys without jobs but even they are parted
By the numbers waiting on their buildings.
Back in the apartment the two bottles there
On the table and she still asleep in the bed
As though no time has passed, she refused it,
Nothing has happened but the empty beer.
It's morning for her but not in the world
That can trade a night for another day
Simply by lifting an invisible hand.
Full morning already, fog in the park
Wreathing the many coming off
The double bridge, each determined again
To block out the thought of four million others
Doing Monday likewise out of sight.

And the cabs that stop almost as often
As they start, bottles packed in crates
On the beds of passing trucks, the rhythm
Causes trivial forgetfulness, white sky.
She leaves her purchase behind in the shop
But it catches her up at the door.

Series

What can one say
About the Little Portion
Friary other than
James Schuyler is
Buried there? It sits
On sixty acres of
Woodland in the heart
Of the wealthiest
Section of Long Island
And whether or not
You mean to encounter
The many frontiers
Of the spiritual life
There's an easily
Defeatable meditation
Maze, fresh bread for sale,
And the entire
Place sets forth
In pastoral complacencies.

Christopher Smart

The ecstatic can visit even in prison
And prison isn't limited. One is
Sent mostly against one's will
To a less than ideal place while in
Ring structures of the body electrical
Impulses play about internally
Uncaring there isn't conservation
Of mental matter. For every choice
Another that could go missing
Never to be thought of. I'm talking about
How economically night descends
How rapidly the opportunity to praise
A friend curls up like a list
Too easy to outlive, why
Among the captures made at night
You still mistake stray sounds
For her feet in frank approach
Nothing but mistakes to make

Themselves taken for investments
Proceeding from years of being near the self-
Cleaning motion in the background
Form of that not yet elegy
Padding about the house. Though innate
I made the prison outside as well
As I could, a play of *for* and *let*
Darks giving way to familiar sight
Of things in their place, light stripes
At the edges then all white underneath
A morning joke whose brightness depends
On its author never being told
It was a garden judgment, that she'd live

A certain amount without ceasing
Then go stopped glass
While nothing else did, so there is
The problem of pertinence, of making
Sure a name is marriage comedy
While also making certain ritual is
No longer the pertinent question
Say she let you be for her, though few
Were admitted to the commission
Of her sound. Say it was enough

To constitute a vertical hymn
Everybody could almost agree
Hovers over the smallest being
Tailored and active, sensible
Through the unreal jacks of the face
Stare long enough and you can see
The arbitrary relation between
Love and its object, the dais of daisy
Spinning within benevolence
The two have a strong relationship
If they are we as we were
They cry out at each other
The history of two orphans who stayed
All summer in a new place
Immediately you feel you have it
You're thinking again of the future
The moment's lost its pentothal
And with it electricity has one fewer
Home. Water under flowing glass
If you want to live again
Put the prefix where the suffix goes

The Names of Production

London Bridge is falling down

ALLEN GROSSMAN

Poetry: A Basic Course

This poem was written at a time when the choice
Was between no choices and one other,
Both repeating daily, as day or in it.
In Spain they were voting to sleep outside,
Talking about their future as though
They could invite it to come be with them.
This poem was written in that time at it,
As if it could invite itself to
Be otherwise. It has the form of a square.

At that time it was raining while Manning
Received letters in her cell. Microloans
Allowed lenders to imagine minor happiness,
Joplin changed. A friend described its

Having sour cherry notes initially
Entirely different when returned to
A few hours later and the poem was
Similar, it had begun in response
To a book about empty persons in poems
Retreating from themselves toward poetry

In the general sense, which makes them
Against the day, in Pynchon's phrase.
It was similar to wine because one had to
Have the privilege of inviting time
To do it, opening its crossings to Gaza
Despite being unfit for trial. It is
An embarrassing poem that chooses words
To stage intentions and the other choice
Just pushes the poem into the stormfront
Of future time, its Spains and Arizonas.

A proper name may be the only word
That can embarrass the poem in the future
As well as the present. It has a life
Of six hundred years before decaying
Into the final broadcast. The choice is thus
Not between no words and words
But the thing between them, a person.

Yet I find it very hard to get ready
In the morning (before 8), especially
If it's summer and the tea tree glows

Like a book you can't yet buy
By any other means. It seems more
And more likely Wilpon will have to
Sell the team, but that's an idle thought
Shared in a private square. The distinction
However is lost on me, sunlight in a book
I failed to finish (not the Izenberg,
The other one), in a time where *I*
And *failed* are synonyms one can't
Choose between so much as move through

Elbowing the others out of my way
To get a better view. But I is also
The others, though not in Ashbery's
Translation—motion may not even be motion
So much as a chain of equivalencies
Posing as bodies, what in poetry
We would call a sight rhyme like that
Between *bury* and *fury*, minor differences,
Those between reading and speaking,
Sleeping and waking, talking while asleep,

Etc., the distinction lost on me
Because of the late May cold in the East
And the summer started so casually
Long before it feels like it has—it was
45 degrees in Chicago during the game
Last night, at the time it was fated
To be, and the game matched this contingency
With its own, which I watched part of
On pirated internet as though I had to.
I hear her upstairs singing this

While exercising, which she's doing again.
Like air traffic over Northern Germany
The poem begins to choose admitting this
Present over refusing to, both does
And doesn't go to the wedding in Kansas,
Accepts what he says about the pomes
Of the quince and redbud while they walk
Through a late Midwestern spring, a loan
Repaid over time. She goes longer and longer,
Mastering her fear of being out of breath,

Falling asleep as the plane takes off,
Unsurprised at the physics, the early hour

With its threats of stagflation and victim
Laws. What I means to say by this is
Each subscription set is $40
But part of what you get is the sense
They're free by the time they come because
You've forgotten paying for them,
And it doesn't hurt that they're slim
Volumes of poetry whose cover never changes

Only the colors of it, a choice within
No choice that mimics the present in a way
I can be upset with or excited by depending
On what time I woke up in what season.
I wanted to do it right this time, a rhyme
Between headline and deadline in a poem
With no endwords but June 1
Approaches through my best I-intentions,
Which mistook bad faith for a real dream

Of falling in love with the not yet
Made as though it were close by,
On the other side of a square you reach
When closing your eyes, invited in
Without having been outside, still

In that grave where anything rhymes.
To be the doom of that effort like
A wheel in the air over Yemen,
Shot again without feeling it for years.
The few readers we promised ourselves

Are us, waiting for time in the general sense.
But days come and the character
With which to measure them unfit
To stand trial. Such that the poem
Is now believed to be the most distant
Object ever seen, a porchlight.
Before he could get there they took
Strauss-Kahn off the plane, no doubt
Alarming other passengers in the process
Of resenting the long trip they had chosen

Freely; Reyes, Wright, and Beltran
Were all classy about it but it isn't summer
Yet, and there is no chance the story will
Wander away—that's why they play the games.
Then one of the volumes comes, by a poet
Who had gone out of her way to be cruel

To me once, but despite this I loved the poem
For its honesty about how little poetry can do
And loved an emptied version of her
For having admitted that in the lonely square

Of a book. I can't even remember whether
This was covered by the last subscription
Or given to me as a gift by the publishers
Because I am just old enough, forty-two
At the time of writing, to function
As a minimal uncle to the words of the young,
The new breath in the pages falling over
Bremen, which only sight-rhymes
With Yemen and has twelve sister cities
Including Durban, Gdańsk, and Haifa.

She is upstairs which means I have no choice
But be downstairs in the present-past,
Which is the difference between affect and effect
Before pronunciation lets you know
Whether either is not the other or a verb
Cleared for takeoff but second in line.
By the time speaking comes you can't remember

Having paid for it so it feels like a gift.
The same holds for waking up in May
On the 25th expecting a fair hearing

From the other I's despite their being pre-
Occupied with a search for the missing.
It's like having to do two interviews
At the same time with one of them
Already late and the other barely started
Though it's now not due till June 10.
No, it *is* that but with the simile still real
As a sister city. All the little others
Who live there like each other does,
Waking up to find that after

Surviving the morning they were faced with
The afternoon is unabated terraces
Already over far to the right. It's undeniable,
More than forty years of collaboration
Both before and during which the body
Was the genius and the life at best
Talented at moving that body around
In time, a poem of the unchosen
Written with the left hand. And previously

This would have been the end, a wan
Gesture designed to melt into air
While May dies, the anticipation
Of freedom rather than its solid world.
But that has come to seem an exercise
In futurity, less an ending than a surrender
To the belief time restarts where a poem
Stops making choices. I'd like simply
To be done with them as at the end of a list
Of proper names—Corinto, Dalian,

Maracaibo, and the rest of Bremen's twins—
But that would be as pale and cold
As the undersides of stones by the Proxy Falls
On a trail through the Three Sisters Wilderness,
One I couldn't find again without help
From the people still minimally there.
It was after the third such accidental strike
That we decided to rebuild our home again
In the intermittent sun, strangers with arms
Linked to protect the thing behind them.

Series

To remember people in the act
Of speaking is to love them
And not the turquoise substrate
Redon supposed was all there was
To vases, any container, the vessel
Objects are. To remember
People in the act of speaking
Is to love them, but not for anything
They say. An open mouth
Unembarrassed in the lower parts
Of the face, vase that when
It's drawn becomes a lamp
Now that it's getting darker
Earlier, done before we are
Finished forgetting not to be,
Thinking about the lip of the vase
Or a smudge of stray indigo
Above it, and the butterfly about
To test the limits of what's happened
Once and less than once.

Six Political Criteria

The world is still for you, the situation
Excellent, there is only a percent
Chance of anything happening.

Never before has our country been
So sliding along its seven days
Without a formula, the well plugged,

House retaken, bargaining done.
We must rise as if to see what is
Really going on among stones

Hunting heaven, in the towers
Hung up again outdoors
Where unmet needs fall back

Into enterprise, others
Delighted the dawn comes up,
That they are there, etc. That

There are bodies and reflections
Of bodies, planes of black glass
In which the heavens disorder

Or order—all things equal
Threats, contradictions that call
For correct handling. But the situation

Excellent for centuries in either
Direction, the border guarded,
Songs sung. We'll want to watch it

Over time, among its honeys
Flowing unobstructedly, clouds
And clouds and clouds, reflections

Of clouds. That they are air
Resolving conflicts peacefully,
Waiting to hear back from.

Why then do some people feel
Each dawn a new issue when
It's been growing and changing

For some time and only now
Sends out flash agents? It is
Sheer fantasy to imagine

New things. There are reflections,
Heavens under other heavens,
Horizons that flow through the streets

In puddles of film. Let a hundred bloom
Like flowers poisonous to sight
There where the sky is grounded,

Where never have so few been
So many disturbances, floods of fact
Spreading answered questions

Across glass, sea surface, century, etc.
Can bad dawns be turned good
Days, given their dual character?

How much time do you have?
We must learn to rise as if
Seeing the inside of horizon

Or not at all. While time is
Dominant but limited, morning
And night the two sides of a single

Problem sunset presses
Together in a discipline
Its reds upset; and through them

Extravagant notions slip
Back into appearances. Folly
Thinking anything superior

To their repeated accumulation
Of gold gone otherwise,
The running dogs with easy

Honey on their backs, large
Fake walls of pleasure's end
Coming apart like agriculture

In the sky. For two years
They worked on this
With *this* and *they*

The least measurable things,
Slow-moving discussions about
How to establish the grounds

A second later never there,
Clouds leaking captures,
Captures growing aftermaths

No one really understands.
The most that can be said is
The end of the assembly is

Provocative: grays edged red
Establishing the primacy of
Color over shape, a sense

Of horizontality worked
Optionally on the inside
Of a shield. What changes how

The sun will lie amid surrendering
Effects, now a bed and now
A valuable exercise in counter-melt,

Yellows bought short, rejected
On the shoulders of the next
Embroidered ray, threads of green

In order beyond number. And
A long gold bank under whites
Of hinted transformation, flushed

Whites opening a cage somewhat
Differently, a west in adequate
Emptiness, the west of the west

In total serration, seven steps
Of a necessary decay
That suits our contradictions.

Winterreise

1

Getting back up without using the arms,
Treating time like a dog or a fog,
A sun detained indefinitely in
The blackout blinds of December,
Unkillable subject, vulnerable body
Standing on the cold stone of Sproul,
In the daily divorce waking wants
To propose, furious mood of everyone
Even nature is willing to perform,
Bees on fire in rosemary camps
Spilling over bricks to a dampness
Not entirely of our making
But perhaps responsible over time
For stretches of asphalt broken like

2

For stretches of asphalt broken like
Design; getting back up suddenly
Just standing there as if always
One had been a living statue
Dawn suffers back into knowledge
A little less suspicious now,
Sleeping on the beach at Far
Rockaway after Zuccotti was cleared,
Where strangers broke out in groups
Whose task is to honor with trouble
An ideal memory of actual May,
The stray cat most important to herself,
The one green centers and keeps warm
Behind all repeated speech

3

Behind all repeated speech
The chest unfolds as nights
Come earlier, movements are discredited,
Raided, snatched and grabbed, to resume
In an echoing term or a wave
Shouting Move while slowly advancing,
Living stream you didn't have to be
There for, half were, false dawn
Or sovereign shatter, holding on
Through the evictable season
Of Santa Anas faking subsiding
Then rising like predictable prosody
Through the paper of the sycamore,
Okay with only passing through

4

Okay with only passing through
Pouring inconsequential powers
At any time from September through March
When high pressure builds over the basin
And in a bodiless chorus passes down
Through channels and canyons, locally
Increasing air speed along the way
Until it arrives with force on your block
Or in the middle of the play, where Hermione says
To me can life be no commodity —
That this was already available to say,
That it's been so long since it was
If it no longer is, to stand up in that
Funny violation of the unities

5

Of the unities the air is patiently
Colored by as though a stranger made it,
Had arrived in the bonded world
Still under construction as Whitman
Would revise a list, adding differences
To sameness while on the edge
Of convergence or horizon;
While art is good, while it arrives
With rich disdain at generosity,
At waiting together in plazas of cold,
Waiting for that cold to deepen
And unpredictably end, come back
Disguised as the we of weekends,
The thou of thousands it takes

6

The thou of thousands it takes
So little to defeat or restore, a thing
Sent back and forth above the brow
While Sunday morning lasts all day,
A complex package of delivery and waste,
A message written over the door,
Weightless meditation on
The accelerando of a song
For occupations, broken ring
Of names and dates no longer used
To put the day back into hours
Where it persistently hangs
Down into distraught spaces
A false dawn steals up from

7

A dawn now come in earnest
Near the unmoving cranes in the port;
And the brittle eucalyptus, what is that
For, mock suns that appear
While walking a narrow ellipse
Across the mouth of Berth 55
On system day, going further
While staying in place, a thing you make
Though already made for you
Like all the raw tales sent up,
Up and down the jagged line
I talked to some of as I endured
Predawn's call for limited visibility,
An insistent tone that waits

8

A litter of tones that waits
For the pattern to break, assume human form
And sound the nervous accusations,
That time has passed since May seemed good
Or it was fair to note the citrus trees,
The lemon in particular doing poorly
For three months now in a climate of
Chilled speech and cannoning sound,
Where Wednesday's gift is Friday's alarm
And all the days are extra days,
Days fundamentally without
Demands, so that their councils would see
How lithe preparedness can get,
Pulling back the blinds, the other

9

Pulling back the blinds, the other
Ones, the entire play of nowhere
In its proper place, inviolable;
Getting back to a natural posture,
Patient with the newcomers, friends
Of these conditions voices are
The bride of, that really could go
Either way rather than entirely
Where yesterday's sharpness fades
On the branch of having to,
A surprise that doesn't go away,
Carries invisible content out
To lure back even the diffident
Who are an old patience becoming

10

Who are an old patience becoming
Atmosphere the mouth will trust
Its emptiness to, can say with the rest
The fence is coming down, came down
And he is safe, wants you to know that
Endless birdsong I dreamt of
Returns to black, stakes the breeze
With acceptable chains, injury
To no one you could be the sign of,
Declared; and each sketch one of many
In a stand-alone series, spring, summer,
Fall with its handle turning toward
The fourth of the cycle as though the first
Three don't belong to me

11

Only the last one does, content to
Wander through the empty bank
As my understanding instructs me
To do, in debt to rich place,
Its prisoner and guest, a face
With all identifying marks removed
On the cover of *Time*; you won't leave
But need reinforcements, three months
As fat as tame things to be ground up
To be gotten through, won across
While the days are called off by each
Inaudible order to disperse
Continually breaking down into
Continually breaking down into

12

Linearly fading; it's summer,
A weekday, and midafternoon, another
Alternate world where Oedipa is
Searching through the footnotes
In a fat book akin to those
You read about, the sort that bring
Governments down, maybe endlessly,
Without anything really changing
At all for the students, still 11:36 a.m.
In Berkeley as the women of Cairo
March to say again to the military
They'll walk with their something to lose
Past the steel reeds, and to say
Hey, I'm tired of dying

The Flagstad Recording

Control has been candied and exchanged
So many times it feels like the night
Of the day, a troubled ride through
A beginning whose motor announces
It's still mild guardian
Of a human bird we don't yet hear.
She needs no protection nor exists
Except as a set of performances,
Notes mistaken for an identity
In sequence, much as we take quiet
Sounds to be an index of their distance
From the only place that matters.
This is not description but paraphrase
The voice does as contradictions,
New but old, certainly uncertain
About the decision to wear white
Though it's long after Labor Day.
In fact it's that other day in September

Never fully over inside the strings,
And this isn't time, more like the world
Premiere of an anticipation
Of an accompaniment that isn't
Paraphrase so much as the last
Chance at exhausted debut.

ACKNOWLEDGMENTS: For their support and suggestions many thanks to John Ashbery, Cal Bedient, Jeff Clark, Timothy Donnelly, Alan Felsenthal, Graham Foust, Judith Goldman, David Gorin, Bob Hass, Lyn Hejinian, Brenda Hillman, Ben Lerner, Eric Linsker, Christopher Miller, Amanda Nadelberg, Joanna Picciotto, the men of San Quentin, and Matthew Zapruder. I am also indebted to Joshua Beckman, Heidi Broadhead, and the rest of Wave for their work on the book.

Grateful acknowledgment is made to the editors and staff of the publications in which versions of these poems appeared: *Better*: "Distraction"; *Boston Review*: "At the Edge of the Bed"; *The Claudius App*: "The Names of Production"; *Critical Quarterly*: "Entheogen," "Tales of Unrest"; *Floor*: "People on Sunday (1930)"; *Gulf Coast*: "Six Political Criteria"; *Lana Turner: A Journal of Poetry and Opinion*: "D'Haussonville," "Winterreise"; Poets.org: "The Flagstad Recording," "From Honey to Ashes"; *Reclamations*: "Thanatopsis"; *The The*: "Suleiman"; and *Wave Composition*: "Christopher Smart," "Mark," "Second Intensity."

Many thanks to Ben Estes and Alan Felsenthal for printing "Hesiod" as a chapbook (*The Song Cave*, 2010). Thanks also to Barbara Claire Freeman for including "Materia" and "Four Last Songs" in *Three Poets* (Minus A Press, 2012).